D1242948

Hello out there!

MESSAGES IN CODE

Janet Weller

Illustrated by Colin Mier

W

FRANKLIN WATTS
A Division of Grolier Publishing
NEW YORK • LONDON • HONG KONG • SYDNEY
DANBURY, CONNECTICUT

© Franklin Watts 1998
First American Edition 1998 by
Franklin Watts, A Division of Grolier Publishing
90 Sherman Turnpike, Danbury, CT 06816
Visit Franklin Watts on the Internet at:
http://publishing.grolier.com

A CIP catalog record for this book is available from the Library of Congress
ISBN: 0-531-14475-5 (lib.bdg)
0-531-15346-0 (pbk)

Series editor: Rachel Cooke
Editor: Sarah Snashall
Designer: Melissa Alaverdy
Picture research: Sue Mennell

Printed in Belgium

Picture acknowledgements:
Cover image: Telegraph Picture Library, all others Steve Shott
AKG Photo, London p. 7 (Julius Gopel); Matt Cooke/Bletchley Park Trust p. 23
Mary Evans Picture Library p. 21t; Hulton Getty Collection p. 17, 26
Hutchison Library p. 14; Image Bank p. 10 (Dann Coffey)
Imperial War Museum p. 21b
Science Photo Library pp. 25 (Paul Shambroom), 29t (David Parker)
Frank Spooner/Gamma pp. 29b (Murdo Macleod)
Telegraph Colour Library pp. 8, 13l, 13r, 27; John Walmsley pp. 4l, 4r

CONTENTS

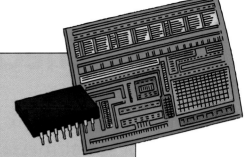
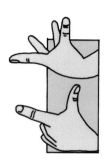

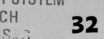

Code Check

When you first think about **codes**, you probably think of secret messages being sent by spies and soldiers in wartime. But these are not the only kinds of codes.

Codes All Around Us

In ordinary life we are surrounded by other kinds of codes, some secret and some not so secret. We probably use some kind of code every day of our lives.

Colors often give us coded messages: red and green traffic lights tell us when to stop or go.

Bar codes carry information about goods in stores.

Different colored flags give messages to racing drivers.

The secret code for this combination lock is used to keep a bicycle safe.

Here someone is typing a special code number into a cash dispenser. If the number matches the code hidden in the shiny strip on the back of the card, the computer will let the person take some money out of their bank account.

LOTTERY

1st MIDWEEK DRAW
HAS A GUARANTEED
10m JACKPOT

A 02 03 13 16 31 42
B 03 07 17 18 42 47
C 01 05 15 17 20 41
D 05 11 12 16 17 30

A lottery ticket carries a coded version of the lottery numbers printed on it.

What Are Codes?

Hmmmm, it says "Meet me urgently outside the bank at 2:30pm."

Codes are ways of passing on information either very quickly or very secretly. One person can change an ordinary message by using a code, and as long as the person who reads the message knows the code, he or she will be able to work out the original message.

Codes and Ciphers

A code is a set of special signs, symbols, numbers, or words that can stand for ordinary letters or words. A special kind of code is called a **cipher**. A cipher either jumbles up the letters of a message or else substitutes different letters or numbers for them. A cipher follows a special rule called a **key**, which controls the way the letters are jumbled or changed. Each cipher has its own key.

HELLO!

In **World War I** a clothesline was used to send Morse code (see page 9). Sheets stood for dashes and pillowcases stood for dots.

Code Beginnings

Codes and ciphers are nearly as old as writing itself. The first codes were carved on **ancient Egyptian** monuments and were probably just for fun. But the need to keep secrets during wars soon meant that codes were used very seriously.

405 BC

A message has just arrived . . .

Give me your belt!

Spartan Code-Sticks

The **Spartans** were a powerful people in **ancient Greece**. They used a special stick called a *scytale* (pronounced to rhyme with Italy) to hide their secret messages.

Don't you want this letter, sir?

No, just your belt!

This scytale message says "danger."

Square Cipher

In ancient Greece, a man named Polybius invented one of the very first ciphers. He wrote the letters of the alphabet in a numbered grid like this:

HELLO!

Polybius used his cipher to signal over long distances by placing groups of huge vases on two walls to show the coordinates!

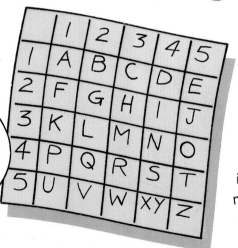

	1	2	3	4	5
1	A	B	C	D	E
2	F	G	H	I	J
3	K	L	M	N	O
4	P	Q	R	S	T
5	U	V	W	X Y	Z

The cipher works a bit like the coordinates on a map. To write the letter H in cipher, you look for H on the grid, then read off the number of the column it is in (3) and then the row (2). So 32 stands for H.

Activity

Make your own *scytale* out of a cardboard tube.

1 Find two tubes of the same size. Give one to a friend.

2 Wrap a long narrow strip of paper tightly around the tube. Hold the ends in place with paper clips.

3 Write a message to your friend on the strip.

4 Unwrap the strip and fill in the gaps with any letters you like.

5 Your friend can **decode** the message by wrapping the strip around their tube.

Caesar's Cipher

The famous **Roman** general **Julius Caesar** used a very simple cipher to send messages to his soldiers. First he would write down two alphabets next to each other like this:

A B C D E F G H I J K L M N O P Q R S T U V W X Y Z
X Y Z A B C D E F G H I J K L M N O P Q R S T U V W

In the **enciphered** message each letter from the top row would be changed into the letter from the bottom row. So:

SEND MORE SUPPLIES   becomes: PBKA JLOB PRMMIFBP

▲ Julius Caesar

Poetic Codes

The ancient Chinese used poems as codes. Before a battle, generals would choose a well-known poem and give each Chinese character in the poem an extra meaning, such as ADVANCE TO THE RIVER. Later, when they wanted to send a secret message they would simply write out the character with the right secret meaning and send that.

Signs and Signals

Before the invention of the telephone and the radio, people had to rely on runners and horse riders to take messages long distances. This could be quite slow, so people invented ways of signaling across great distances. They used coded signs that were not very secret but that could only be understood by people who knew the code.

Fire Signs

In many parts of the world people used smoke signals by day and fires by night to send their messages. They would agree in advance what the smoke or fire meant.

All at Sea

Sailors sometimes use the **International Flag Code** to send messages from their ship to other ships nearby. Although most ships now communicate by radio, flags can still be useful when sailors want to signal to someone who speaks a different language.

The flags for the letters **N** and **C** mean "I am in distress and need immediate help."

▲ C

◀ N

Morse Code

Morse code, invented in 1867 by Samuel Morse, uses groups of dots and dashes to stand for the letters of the alphabet.

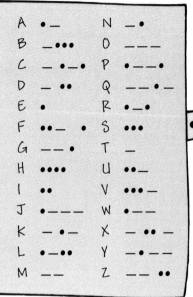

A	• —	N	— •
B	— • • •	O	— — —
C	— • — •	P	• — — •
D	— • •	Q	— — • —
E	•	R	• — •
F	• • — •	S	• • •
G	— — •	T	—
H	• • • •	U	• • —
I	• •	V	• • • —
J	• — — —	W	• — —
K	— • —	X	— • • —
L	• — • •	Y	— • — —
M	— —	Z	— — • •

These dots and dashes were turned into long and short electrical signals and sent along a telegraph wire. At the other end the signals would be turned back into dots and dashes on a strip of paper and "read" by a telegraph operator.

Survival Signs

If travelers become stranded in a remote part of the world like Antarctica or the desert, they can use special survival signs to signal to passing planes. They can make large versions of these shapes out of rocks and tree branches laid out on a clear piece of ground so that a pilot can spot them easily.

Some survival signs and their meanings:

☐   —   F

Require map and compass   Require doctor   Require food and water

HELLO!

Morse code can be used as a distress signal (SOS) by flashing long and short flashes with a flashlight.

Picture Codes

You can use pictures, colors, and symbols to send coded messages. Colors are especially good for giving simple information very quickly. Picture messages can also be much safer than written ones. An enemy will usually ignore something that looks like a meaningless drawing or shape.

Color Codes

Color codes are used to send messages many different ways:

▲ To tell a racing driver when he has won a race.

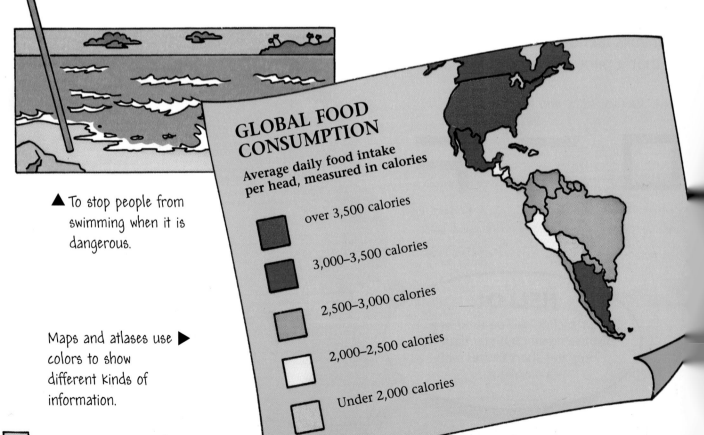

▲ To stop people from swimming when it is dangerous.

Maps and atlases use ▶ colors to show different kinds of information.

GLOBAL FOOD CONSUMPTION

Average daily food intake per head, measured in calories

■ over 3,500 calories

■ 3,000–3,500 calories

■ 2,500–3,000 calories

□ 2,000–2,500 calories

□ Under 2,000 calories

Fancy Passports

In the 17th century, **King Louis XIV** of France gave special picture-coded passports to visitors to his country. Each passport carried a lot of coded facts about the person who owned it. So if a person was carrying a stolen passport, the king's ministers would know right away.

An oval shape meant that the holder was between 45 and 55 years of age.

Green meant the holder of the passport was Russian.

Different flowers showed whether a person was a friend to the state or not.

These lines showed the holder's height and weight.

These patterns showed a person's religion.

A ribbon showed whether the person was married or not.

A Louis XIV passport
(artist's impression)

Ivan Pullofski

Coded Cards

Card cheats add secret marks to the designs on the backs of playing cards. The marks are coded to show the different values of the cards: ace, king, queen, and so on.

Can you spot the difference between these two playing cards? The marked card is on the left.

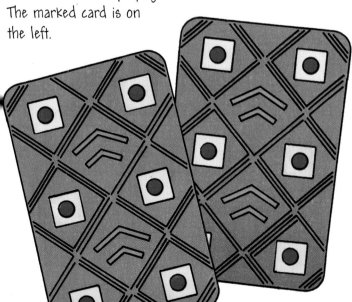

CIPHERTEXT!

This sketch of a butterfly was made by a spy. It is really a map showing the size of a fortress and the positions of some large guns.

Activity

Draw a picture that has a secret map hidden in it for your friend. Draw the map first and then think of a picture that would fit around it.

Hidden Messages

Sometimes it is easier to hide a secret message than to put it into code. You can either put your message in an unusual place, or else make it very small or invisible.

A Code in the Head

An ancient Greek ambassador in Persia sent information home to Greece in a very secret way. He shaved his slave's head and branded a secret message on the man's scalp. When the slave's hair had grown again, the ambassador sent him back to Greece. The Greeks shaved off the slave's hair and revealed the message.

HELLO!

During **World War II** private letters were checked by officials for secret messages. Knitting patterns and lists of football scores were removed in case they contained coded numbers.

Secret Writing

Spies use special inks, made from chemicals, that are invisible until different chemicals are added to them. For example, iron sulfate makes an ink that is invisible until it is painted over with potassium cyanate. Together the two chemicals turn bright blue.

CIPHERTEXT!

Some secret agents owned special pairs of socks that had been soaked in chemicals. When the spies rinsed their socks, they could make invisible ink from the water!

Minute Microdots

Microdots are very small photographs of secret documents. To make a microdot, a document is photographed again and again with a special camera until the picture is on a tiny piece of film – smaller than 1 mm. A microdot can be disguised as a period in an ordinary letter or stuck underneath a stamp.

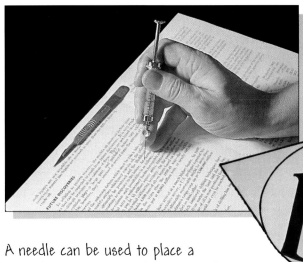

A needle can be used to place a microdot onto a page of writing, and a scalpel may be used to remove it.

Activity

You can make your own secret ink out of lemon juice.

1 Write a message to a friend using lemon juice for ink and the end of a used matchstick as a pen.

Jo Dunn
12 River Way
New York
USA

2 When the message is dry, send it to your friend.

3 Your friend can make the message reappear by holding it next to a warm lightbulb or ironing it with a warm iron. (Get a grown-up to help with this.)

Come to my party on Sunday

Sound Signals

Codes and signals can be heard as well as seen or read. Drums, bugles, whistles, and even special kinds of songs have been used to send messages over long distances. We can speak in code too; pilots as well as spies use coded phrases and passwords to send messages and identify themselves to each other.

Talking Drums

For many years African tribes used the sounds of special drums to send messages that foreigners could not understand.

Different parts of an African "talking" drum make different tones when hit. In some African languages each spoken word has a special pattern of low and high tones – a sort of tune. Drummers can bang these tunes on the drum and make their drums talk. The drums can be heard by tribes living several miles away.

Whistling Codes

Whistling can also be used to send messages. On the mountainous island of La Gomera, off the coast of Africa, people still use a prehistoric whistling language to send messages across the steep valley sides. Sports referees use whistles to signal to players when to start and stop play.

CIPHERTEXT!

In World War II **Navajo** people from North America worked as radio operators. They sent secret military messages in the Navajo language, because very few people apart from Navajos could understand it.

Morse Code

Soon after its invention, the dots and dashes of Morse code (see page 9) were turned into long and short beeps that could be sent by telegraph wire and later by radio. Morse code signals were easier to send clearly by radio than the human voice, and Morse code itself could be disguised with a cipher.

◀ Telegraph wire.

Someone tapping out a ▼ Morse code message.

▲ Someone receiving the message in Morse code.

HELLO!

During World War II, BBC radio broadcasts included personal messages to families at the end of news bulletins. Some of these family greetings were really coded messages to secret agents working in **Occupied France**.

Spies and Lies

There are many kinds of spies and secret agents, and all of them use codes. Some agents go to foreign countries to find out secret information; others stay at home and try to catch **traitors** and foreign agents working in their own country. Being a spy like **James Bond** can sound exciting, but many spies have lived dangerous lives that sometimes ended in death.

A Royal Code

In 1586 **Mary, Queen of Scots,** wanted the throne of England for herself. She and her friends were plotting to get rid of the queen of England, **Queen Elizabeth I.**

1 Unfortunately Mary was a prisoner in her own house.

2 A friend of Mary's named Gilbert Gifford sent her letters secretly by putting them in barrels.

3 Mary read the letter, then put a coded reply into another barrel.

4 But Gifford was a **double agent** who was really working for Queen Elizabeth's minister, Sir Francis Walsingham.

5 A man called Thomas Phelippes could decode Mary's letters. He sent coded messages to Mary's friends pretending they were from her.

6 Soon Mary's friends were arrested and Mary herself lost her life.

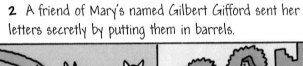

Sir Francis, Here are letters written by Mary.

When Queen
Lla Ho :LHH·o
HRo+bgH+a oᴅ
mHbm ta꜀Howxoн
ᴅom bH+aн oRHH
oᴅRo ᴅ+ᴌbR+

▲ This code says: "When Queen Elizabeth is dead, then come and set me free. Mary Stuart."

Civil Spies

Many of the spies who worked during the **American Civil War** were women. One of the most famous was Rose O'Neal Greenhow. She spied on important people in the North and sent secret information to a colonel in the South. At one time Rose had a network of about 50 spies working for her, most of them women.

After a while, Rose was arrested and put in prison, but she continued to control her spy network from behind bars.

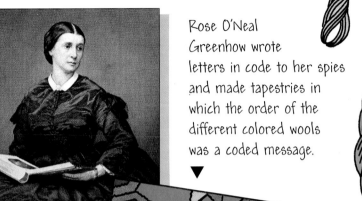

Rose O'Neal Greenhow wrote letters in code to her spies and made tapestries in which the order of the different colored wools was a coded message. ▼

A Double Life

A spy often has to live as a completely different person in order to be successful. In 1962 Elie Cohen began spying for Israel against Syria. Before that he spent a year in Argentina "becoming" a rich Syrian businessman. He then went to live in Damascus with his new name and identity. He made friends with many important Syrian people.

Cohen found out secret information about the Syrian armed forces and sent it back to Israel by radio. Unfortunately he made the mistake of sending too many coded radio messages. The Syrians used a radio direction finding machine to track down his radio, and he was arrested.

AGENT NO: 228
COVER: Businessman
BIRTH NAME: Elie Cohen
YEAR OF BIRTH: 1924
BIRTHPLACE: Egypt

TOP SECRET

HELLO!
Double agents are spies who appear to be working for one country or side but are really spying for the other. An agent named Juan Pujol was so successful at this that he was given medals by both sides!

Secret Lives

Sometimes groups of people want to keep their activities undercover because they are being persecuted, or because they are criminals, or just because they like being secret. These secret societies often use secret signs, codes, and enciphered writing.

The Fish of the Faithful

Some of the Christians who lived in ancient Rome were persecuted by the emperor, so they had to hold their meetings in secret. They used a simple drawing of a fish to tell other Christians where they were.

The fish was chosen as a symbol because the letters of the Greek word for fish, **ICHTHUS**, stood for the words of a phrase about Jesus:

CIPHERTEXT!

Early Christians in Roman Britain decorated the walls of the rooms where they worshiped with coded word puzzles that hid secret writing about their religion.

This fish symbol ring could be shown secretly to another Christian.

I	CH	TH	U	S
Iesous	Christos	Theou	Uios	Soter
Jesus	Christ	God's	Son	Savior

Criminal Codes

Secret gangs in China and India sometimes used coded hand signals to pass on secret messages to other gang members. These signals looked like ordinary everyday movements.

Indian coded hand signals, from left to right: "I am a priest," "Let's talk in private," and "Don't attack."

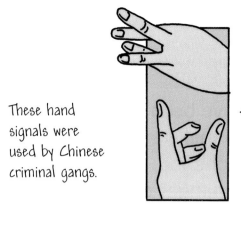

These hand signals were used by Chinese criminal gangs.

◀ These two signs show that some money has been correctly paid.

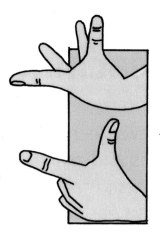

◀ These two signs show that some money has been received.

Total Secrecy

The society of the Rosicrucians is so secret that very few facts are known about it. The society started in the middle ages. Their beliefs may be a mixture of ancient Egyptian cults, Arabian mysticism, and Christianity.

Rosicrucians are supposed to cure the sick without asking for payment and to give money to governments so that they can care for their citizens better.

HELLO!
Rosicrucians have claimed that they feel neither hunger nor thirst, and that they could become invisible and control spirits!

◀ "Rosicrucians" written in cipher.

R O S I C R U C I A N S

ABC	DEF	GHI
JKL	MNO	PQR
STU	VWX	YZ

◀ The Rosicrucians used this cipher grid for some of their secret writings.

Read the cipher message above. Can you guess how the cipher works?

A few people today still claim to belong to the Rosicrucian society, but they do not like to talk about themselves and their beliefs.

Cipher Machines

Ever since the seventeenth century, people have been inventing devices and machines to help them make and crack ciphers. These machines can make enciphering much quicker and easier, but there is still the danger of the cipher machine falling into the hands of the enemy.

Alberti's Cipher Disc

An Italian named Leon Battista Alberti invented the first simple cipher machine in 1466. This is how his "cipher disc" works:

The letter **A** on the small disc is next to **U** on the large disc, so **A** in the message becomes **U** in the code.

Y becomes **S**, and so on...

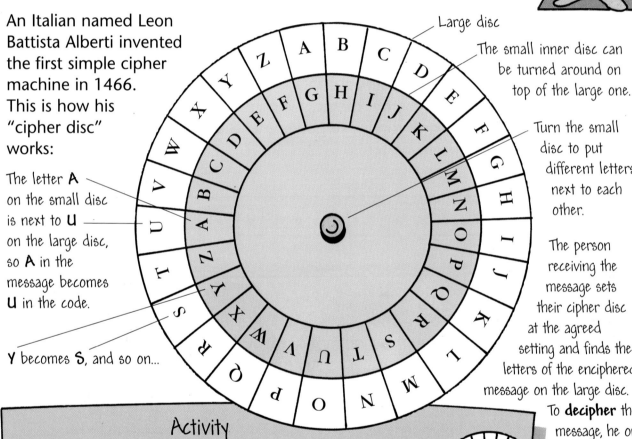

Large disc

The small inner disc can be turned around on top of the large one.

Turn the small disc to put different letters next to each other.

The person receiving the message sets their cipher disc at the agreed setting and finds the letters of the enciphered message on the large disc.

To **decipher** the message, he or she reads off the letters next to them on the small disc.

Activity

Make your own cipher disk. Use it to write a message for your friend and see if he or she can solve it.

1 Cut out two card discs, one 4 in across, one 3 in across. Write the alphabet around the edge of both.

2 Place the small disc on top of the bigger disc and fix them together through the middle with a paper fastener.

The President's Cipher

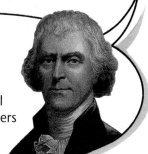

HELLO!
Unfortunately Jefferson put his new invention in a desk drawer and forgot about it. It wasn't until the 20th century that wheel ciphers were reinvented.

In the eighteenth century, **Thomas Jefferson**, who later became president of the United States, invented a brilliant machine called a wheel cipher. This machine had 25 discs, each with the alphabet on it in a different order.

Each disc can be rotated.

1 Line up the discs to show the message you want to send..

2 Write down another line of letters from alongside. For example: ▶

Z L P V O B V S Z P L I J B P U V I Q O J U V N P

3 Send this as the enciphered message.

4 The person who receives the message lines up these letters on their wheel cipher, then finds the real message on another row.

Enigmatic Ciphers

During World War II, Germany used an amazing cipher machine called the **Enigma** machine which looked like a strange typewriter. Inside it were several wheels, or rotors, with the alphabet on them – a little like Jefferson's wheel cipher.

When a letter was pressed on the keyboard, another letter would light up on the panel above. This letter was the cipher letter. Several different rotors could be put into the machine in different positions, and the electric plugs could be connected in many different ways. This meant that the cipher letters changed millions of times, making Enigma, the German cipher machine, almost impossible to break.

Breaking a Code

Lots of clever codes and ciphers have been invented in the past. Every time someone thought up a new cipher, they said it was absolutely unbreakable and would always be a secret. But most codes and ciphers contain some clues to the real message and most codes and ciphers are eventually broken.

How to Break a Cipher

In languages that use alphabets, some letters are used much more often than others. The Arabs were the first people to notice this about Arabic, and in 1412 a writer named Al Qalqashandi realized how useful this knowledge could be if you wanted to break a cipher. In English, for example, the letter E is used the most often. The next most oftenly used is T.

Breaking a Simple Cipher

Here is a message in cipher. In it the letters that appear most often are B and Q:

B appears nine times and Q appears four times, so every B could stand for E and every Q for T. In fact, they do!

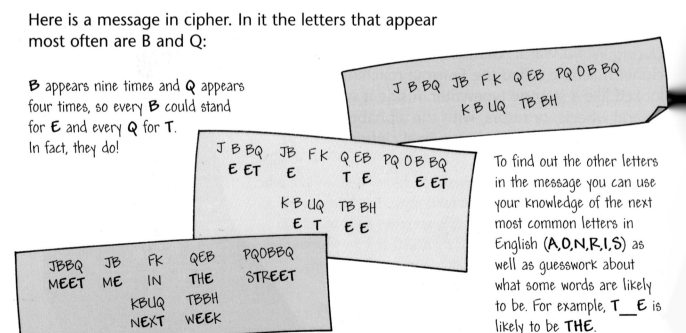

JBBQ JB FK QEB PQOBBQ
KBUQ TBBH

JBBQ JB FK QEB PQOBBQ
E ET   E   T E   E ET
KBUQ TBBH
E T   E E

JBBQ   JB   FK   QEB   PQOBBQ
MEET   ME   IN   THE   STREET
KBUQ   TBBH
NEXT   WEEK

To find out the other letters in the message you can use your knowledge of the next most common letters in English (A, O, N, R, I, S) as well as guesswork about what some words are likely to be. For example, T_E is likely to be THE.

Superhuman Code Breaking

The **code breakers** who wanted to break the Enigma ciphers (see page 21) had to find out the original starting positions – or settings – of the rotors on the Enigma machine.

They knew these settings would help them solve the Enigma messages for one day. First they used their code-breaking skills to try to work out the most likely rotor settings for a group of messages. But checking all the possible rotor settings was an impossibly slow process. Machines called "bombes" were invented to find the right rotor settings quickly.

A team of people was needed to decipher the Enigma code each day. These women are working at "consoles" recording the correct settings for the day's Enigma code.

Colossus

In 1943 a mathematician named Alan Turing invented a super-bombe, which worked much faster than the ordinary bombes. This was the world's first electronic computer, codenamed **Colossus**. Colossus helped solve the Enigma ciphers much more quickly.

A modern reconstruction of Colossus. ▶

Computer Codes

Computers work by using a special code called **binary code**. Binary code turns all kinds of information – even pictures, voices, and music – into combinations of binary digits, which computers find easy to deal with.

Bits and Pieces

All the data and instructions in computers are stored as numbers made up of the digits 0 and 1.

The binary digits — 0 and 1 — are called **bits**.
▼

Binary code is a different way of writing numbers from the decimal numbers we use everyday. Here is 19 written in decimal numbers and in binary code:

Decimal number 19 ▼

1000s	100s	10s	1s
		1	9

Binary code 19 ▼

64	32	16	8	4	2	1
		1	0	0	1	1

Bits are changed into signals, or pulses of electricity, that are either on or off: an "on" pulse is 1; an "off" pulse is 0.

These pulses can be combined into millions of different patterns of on and off. The computer uses these patterns of pulses to add, subtract, compare, memorize, and process lots of information.

These on/off switches show how the binary code for 19 becomes a pattern of electronic signals.

HELLO!

A modern car key can now be coded so that it is recognized by the car's computer system. Each time the key is turned in the ignition, the key and the computer "agree" on a new code number. If the wrong key is put in next time, it will not give the agreed code number, the computer will not recognize it, and the car will not start.

Chip Codes

The invention of the silicon chip, or **microchip**, meant that computer technology could be put into all kinds of everyday machines. Computers in these machines use special codes to help them process information.

▲ A silicon chip with and without its protective casing.

Calculators, washing ▶ machines, and keyboards are everyday machines that have microchips.

The patterns of light and dark on a bar code are changed into electronic signals that send information about a product to the computer. ▶

178063 1577931

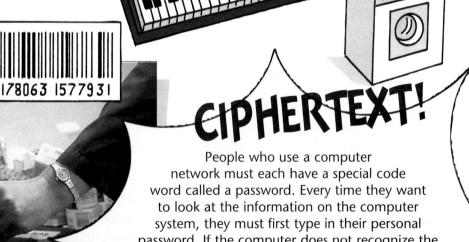

▲ A scanner "reads" the pattern of the bar code and changes it into electronic signals.

CIPHERTEXT!

People who use a computer network must each have a special code word called a password. Every time they want to look at the information on the computer system, they must first type in their personal password. If the computer does not recognize the password, they are not allowed to look at any information on the network.

Unbreakable Codes?

Is there really such a thing as an unbreakable code or cipher?

W	O	N	D	E
R	F	U	L	A
B	C	G	H	I/J
K	M	P	Q	S
T	V	X	Y	Z

The Playfair cipher was invented by Charles Wheatstone, a Victorian scientist.

Playfair

One clever cipher that is very difficult to break is the Playfair cipher. Playfair uses a secret key word and a grid of letters like this.

The keyword "wonderful" is filled in on the grid followed by the unused letters of the alphabet in order.

1 First, the message is divided into pairs of letters:

TH/EY/HA/VE/BE/EN/CA/UG/HT.

2 Find the first pair, **TH**, on the grid.

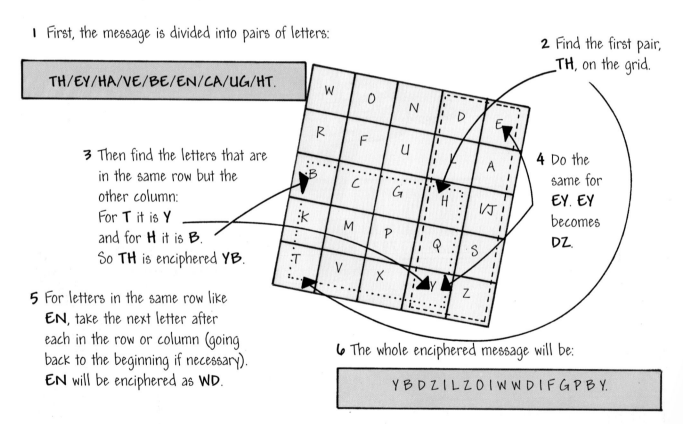

3 Then find the letters that are in the same row but the other column:
For **T** it is **Y** and for **H** it is **B**.
So **TH** is enciphered **YB**.

4 Do the same for **EY**. **EY** becomes **DZ**.

5 For letters in the same row like **EN**, take the next letter after each in the row or column (going back to the beginning if necessary). **EN** will be enciphered as **WD**.

6 The whole enciphered message will be:

YBDZILZOIWWDIFGPBY.

The only way to break a Playfair cipher is to look at the pairs of letters that appear together. In many languages some pairs of letters often appear together. In English for example, **th** and **he** occur together in many different words. Knowing what these common pairs of letters are can help you break a Playfair cipher.

An Unbreakable Cipher

One truly unbreakable cipher system is the onetime pad. A onetime pad has lots of sheets of large random numbers. Each sheet has different numbers on it. Each sheet is used only once.

The message can only be deciphered by someone who has a copy of the same onetime pad.

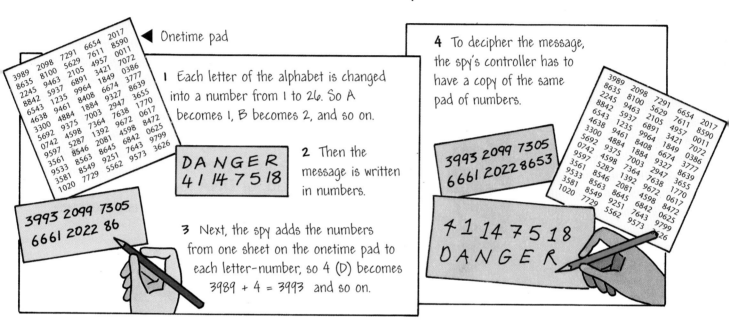

◀ Onetime pad

1 Each letter of the alphabet is changed into a number from 1 to 26. So A becomes 1, B becomes 2, and so on.

DANGER
4 1 14 7 5 18

2 Then the message is written in numbers.

3 Next, the spy adds the numbers from one sheet on the onetime pad to each letter-number, so 4 (D) becomes 3989 + 4 = 3993 and so on.

3993 2099 7305
6661 2022 86

4 To decipher the message, the spy's controller has to have a copy of the same pad of numbers.

3993 2099 7305
6661 2022 8653

41 14 7 5 18
DANGER

Person enciphering with a onetime pad.

Person deciphering with a onetime pad.

Super Ciphers

Most modern ciphers are made by special computer programs. Computers can encipher messages using complicated mathematical processes. To unscramble these modern ciphers you need a lot of computer power and the right deciphering program.

CIPHERTEXT!

Sometimes ciphers can be disguised as **digitized** computer pictures so you can't even see them!

27

The Code of Life

A special kind of code is the basis of all life on Earth. This is the **genetic code** – the code of nature. The reason we look like our parents and grandparents is because they have passed the color of our hair and our eyes to us in the form of **genes**: a gene for hair color, a gene for eye color, and so on. Genes are passed on in the form of a code.

The Genetic Code

In this natural code, small chemical pieces join together in many different ways to make different genes. These genes are carried on a substance called deoxyribonucleic acid, or **DNA** for short. Our parents pass on combinations of their DNA to us when we are born.

DNA looks like a twisted rope ladder.

To pass on genes, DNA splits down the middle. Each half can copy itself again exactly.

Can you see which genes these parents have passed to their children?

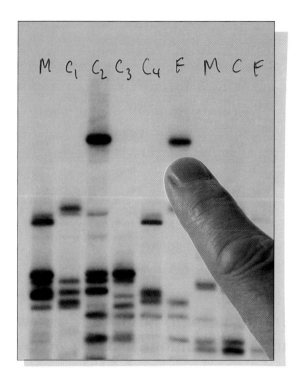

Follow the Code

Each person's genetic code is unique. The police can use this code to track down criminals. They can take samples of blood or saliva from the scene of a crime, analyze the DNA, and find the code for one person. They can match this code to the codes in blood samples taken from suspects.

DNA can be used to prove that people are related. In the photograph, each band relates to a different gene. By comparing family groups you can see which gene each child (C) inherited from each parent (M and F).

HELLO!
In 1997 scientists created the first **cloned** sheep; they used the DNA from one sheep to make another sheep with exactly the same DNA.

Cracking the Code of Life

Scientists have now learned to change DNA. This could bring amazing new advances in medicine and science. For example, diseases that until now have been incurable might be curable because scientists will be able to remove or change the genes that cause them.

New types of plants can now be **genetically engineered** – plants designed to grow in barren parts of the world or resist pests.

Useful Words

American Civil War: (1861–1865) A war fought between the Northern and Southern states of North America.

ancient Egyptians: a people who lived in Egypt about 5,000 years ago. They built the pyramids. Their civilization lasted for about 3,000 years.

ancient Greeks: The ancient Greeks lived in Greece from about 1000 BC until 146 BC. Their civilization is the basis of modern Western science and thought.

bar code: A row of thick and thin black lines that store information. Bar codes are used by stores to give information to cashiers about price. They are also often used on library books.

binary code: A numbering system based on the digits 0 and 1 that is used by computers to process information.

bit: A binary digit – 0 or 1. Bits are the basic elements of computer code.

Bond, James: A famous spy in books and films who was created by the writer Ian Fleming.

Caesar, Julius (100 BC–44 BC): A famous Roman general who became a great Roman leader. During his rise to power, he fought many battles.

cipher: A way of changing a piece of writing by jumbling up the letters or else substituting different letters or numbers for them. A cipher has a key.

clone: A living thing, plant or animal, that has exactly the same genetic makeup (DNA) as another living thing.

code: A set of special signs, symbols, numbers, or words that can stand for ordinary letters, numbers, or words.

code breaker: Someone who solves codes and ciphers.

Colossus: The world's first electronic computer. It was invented by Alan Turing to crack the German Enigma ciphers.

DNA: Deoxyribonucleic acid – the chemical that is the basis of all life.

decipher: To change a piece of enciphered writing back into real words.

decode: To change a piece of coded writing back into real words.

digitized: Made up of binary digits.

double agent: A spy who is working for two opposing sides at the same time.

Elizabeth I (1533–1603): Queen of England from 1558 until 1603.

encipher: To change a piece of writing using a cipher.

Enigma: A cipher machine used by Germany during World War II.

gene: A length of coded DNA which controls a human characteristic, e.g. black hair, blue eyes.

genetic code: The way in which chemicals combine in different ways to make different genes.

genetically engineered: A plant or animal is genetically engineered if it has had its genes altered or added to by scientists.

International Flag Code: A code used by ships to signal to each other.

Jefferson, Thomas (1743–1826): Third president of the United States of America. He was also a keen inventor and designer.

key: A special rule that controls the way the letters are jumbled up or substituted in a cipher. For example, writing letters in a numbered grid and using the coordinates of the squares instead of the letters.

King Louis XIV: A king of France who ruled from 1643 until 1715.

Mary, Queen of Scots (1542–1587): A queen of Scotland who tried to become queen of England in place of Elizabeth I.

microchip: A small silicon chip used to give computer power to everyday machines.

microdot: A tiny photograph of a secret document, so small it can be disguised as a period.

Morse code: A code made up of dots and dashes, invented by Samuel Morse for sending messages by telegraph and later by radio.

Navajo: A tribal people of North America.

Occupied France: The part of France that was occupied by the German army during World War II between 1940 and 1945. During this time, many French people fought an underground resistance to the German occupation.

Romans: An ancient people whose capital was Rome in Italy from 500 BC until AD 400.

Spartans: A people who lived in the south of ancient Greece. They were famous for their toughness.

traitor: Someone who gives away the secrets of their own country or side to an enemy.

World War I: A war fought by many countries of the world from 1914 until 1918. Britain, France, Italy, Russia, and the United States fought Germany, Austria-Hungary, and Turkey.

World War II: A war fought by many countries of the world from 1939 until 1945. Britain, the Soviet Union, and the United States fought Germany.

Index